With Access to Tools

Poems

With Access to Tools

Poems

Dana Wildsmith

LAKE DALLAS, TEXAS

FIRST EDITION

Requests for permission to reprint or reuse material from this work
should be sent to:

Permissions
Madville Publishing
PO Box 358
Lake Dallas, TX 75065

Cover Design by Kimberly Davis
Cover Photo by Olivier Le Queinec for Shutterstock
Author Photo by Don Wildsmith

ISBN: 9781956440379 paperback, 9781956440386 ebook
Library of Congress Control Number: 2022944383

For Wesley Scoates
and all the Scoates men who were and are masters of tools
And to the memory of Terry Kay

Contents

III. Tools for Mind and Body

With Access to Tools

Poems

I.

Tools for Home and Garden

How to Sing

To praise my tools, I wear them out. My hoe's
blunt tip is history in 2/2 time,
a simple chopping meter down the rows
of years that rose and fell like breathing. I'm
not finished yet. Whoever is? The work
that weeded me still needs me keeping watch
for what should grow and what should not. The dark,
the daze, the drench, the drought. I doubt I've brought
to fruit two-thirds of what I've planted—dreams,
a child, two dogs for every decade—roots
at last on this old farm I seed and weed
each spring as if it mattered. I love my tools
like friends deep-rooted through our history,
rounding out another year with me.

Sighting

When Calvin Edwards ran his cattle fence,
he kept an eye to depth and spacing, not
to how I'd see his fence posts as they lost
a century of cellulose to winds
and August storms teasing out their grain.
Each walk, I see a little less of post
and more of swoops and swirls that cost
the post's integrity but let it gain
a sculpted loveliness that rests in what's
not there. The years between the farmer's days
and mine ghost those hollows time has made
in Mr. Edwards' work. Sometimes I stop
and sight a line from weathered post to post,
cinching then to now through what's been lost.

History

Some dirt should stay. Not every tool should be
wiped clean. Not every day can be resolved
like math or music to a major key,
but that's okay. Today, the mulch I hauled
has snagged in bits and twigs by quitting time,
caught fast to drips of concrete Daddy mixed
before my time. His wheelbarrow is mine,
his legs like iron, his heart beats hit or miss,
his way of plowing through his days as if
each hour caught fire behind him. Days like today
he's there as I lug lime and sand to mix
with rhythmic shovel chops, a messy spray
of mortar melding to the handles where
our hands will hold again on what's left there.

Seed Starter, February

I'm planting hope midway this bleakest month,
this bleakest season. Such a daunting slog
it's been since summer, tending injuries
in friends, nursing injuries from friends.
I knew I needed something like a sun
today to burn away this haunting fog
of weariness that lately hinders me
from seeing where to go or where I've been.
Today, the climate I created when
I seeded broccoli to sprout in pots
beneath a buzzing sun will soothe me
like a walk along a beach in sand
just warming toward a spring I wouldn't swear
could come until I planted hope right here.

Rain Barrel

It gives direction to the flow that comes
sometimes sporadically. It stores the gift
of excess for those drier times when none
of all the tricks of trade you've taught yourself
can compensate for what should be assured
but obviously isn't, always. Here's
where you can serve yourself when nature lets
you down. This fount of smugness, your reserve
replenishment given like a trust,
unearned, found money when all you've grown
is dying on the vine. Wealth is just
to know you have enough to save what's sown
with this stout receptacle of second chance.

Spirit Level

Well, that's the tricky part—to work to keep
your spirit level while the world rocks forth
and back, but not as far back as before.
Close enough's not good enough to meet
without a gap that lets in light. You want
time's lovely bubble resting steady where
you were before you knew a world could veer
off-kilter, tipping to a niggling slant
you still can't rectify. Don't try. Accept
what doesn't compromise integrity.
I mean, don't sweat the small discrepancies.
A level's built to bobble right to left
a teeny bit as circumstance demands.
The trick's to keep the balance in your hands.

Ladder

I'm climbing a stairway to heaven. No, I'm not.
I step again. Now I stop. This step,
then stop. Again. Again. Step and stop.
One more. But never step on top, it says.
Why not? I've earned that utmost spot where I
might see the pitch of roof entire, then snag
the clot of broken branches there, up high.
I wouldn't have to cling and reach and drag
the branches with a rake that breaks the weave
of leaves and limbs and ants to rain on me
and clump my hair with tree debris. I'd leave
the sanctioned step, step up, and waver, free.
No. That reckless step could cost more than it's worth.
My heaven is a place on Earth.

Garden Hoe

It's not as sharp as it used to be. I hear
friends say the same of themselves, but I
believe I've grown sharper through my years
of gardening, at least in ways that I
consider worthy. Now I notice where
my herb beds migrate to and feed the dirt
accordingly. I've learned if nothing's there,
amend or move along. It never hurts
to sow for your own needs, plus more to share.
I've also learned a drought can lend
you time to think and plan, that rain repairs
so quickly you forgive the wait, and when
to be as blunt as my old chopping hoe.
Or when to plow loss under, let it go.

Hammer

Find one that fits your hand. Make no mistake,
you'll know it when you heft it—the way this head
exactly counterbalances its weight
against your fist; the way this handle rests
between your target and your grip just
as truly as the shafts of bone between
your elbow and your wrist. You can trust
this one, so pick it up, extend your reach,
amend your reach's impact. It's part of you,
but more than you. Its verberations last
a little longer than its whack. Can you
not feel it now? The way this hammer gives
your pounding a surprising clout,
like words you said and then forgot about.

Swing Blade

It feels so blessed good to whack a swath
through knee-high weeds one-handed, leading with
your whole right side, hard to an inward swing
and then the swooping follow-through that flings
a ream of severed heads to who cares where.
Just leave them lay. It's not the time to clear
what's cut. Not yet. Keep plowing through
those ankle-twisters that have stymied you
till now. Suddenly, the other side
is worth the getting there. Too long, you've tried
to find your way around this boundless mess;
now straight ahead's the only option left.
It's good to bushwhack through the thick of it,
get rid of this morass. It's good to sweat.

Rubber Mallet

For those occasions when we need to wham
the daylights gently out of rusted bolts
or paving bricks or bumbleheads. We hold
to courtesy here in the South. To name
a fool a fool outright would just be rude.
We bless their hearts, instead, consigning them
the heft of our disdain by inference,
politely put them in their place for good.

Sometimes the softest tap can leave a mark.
I've known a hundred souls come home from war
to ever-after fighting in their minds. The more
we pound, the more they break apart.
We bless their hearts, instead, invoking God
to grasp and put in place what they cannot.

Seam Ripper

I've given them as gifts, those lovely ones
with hand-turned chubby handles veined in orange
and scarlet from a craft shop with a range
of tools made pretty. I'm not making fun—
it pleases me to mix utility
with beauty, but the one I keep for my own
use is plastic, brown, and homely. Why?
Because my grandmother made quilts, she
told me ten stitches to the inch was her
intent—eight or nine was sloppy work
she'd rip right out, she said. I never saw
her use her plastic seam ripper. Small
and careful holds, she said. Stitch to bind
the first time. Watch your needle. Take your time.

Cast Iron Skillet

For cooking or conking. All the old cartoons
and silent comedies spun their laughs
around a harried housewife who had had
enough of her man's sorry ass, so swung
her frying pan to knock some sense in him
or to skedaddle him. Either way worked fine
to give her peace and quiet for a time.
The movies never showed her fetch her pan
from where it fell, regard it as a friend
who understands that love's a recipe
you sometimes have to tweak a bit
to keep its flavors high. She'd study her iron pan
and mind the varied uses of a tool:
to whack a rat or feed a long-loved fool.

Milking Stool

A slab of scrap he sawed to sitting width,
hand-augured holes, four legs jammed at a slant,
that's it. I imagine him flipping it to sit,
then scoot the stool and lean his head, his hands,
against her belly soft as wood worn smooth
from sixty years of sitting by the time
the stool was mine. I never saw it used,
never met the man who made it. I'm
a gardener, not a farmer. Never milked
a cow or wanted to. I grab his stool
to prop my feet on while I sit and talk
with four fat cats about the usual:
how evening's milky light burnishes their fur
as tawny as old wood, but lovelier.

Door

I'd rather have a door that I could shut
to keep my morning space unoccupied, but
with someone always on the other side to meet
me there halfway between my wants and needs
mid-day when I've exhausted those first thoughts
that first light chases out like creatures caught
between another world and mine. I want
to bide my time in pondering but can't.
I never can. By noon, I need relief
from what's inside, or what's outside needs me.

And that's what doors are for. A door provides
an easy out when mystery collides
with what my mind can translate into words,
or should. When whispers only I have heard
beguile me most, an open door can end
the spell and save me for the world again.

Comealong

I likely love the name more than the tool,
too scary with its risk of snapping back,
its ratchet clacking as the chain unspools
so wildly every uncle snatches back
his hand in every memory—*woo, Lord*—
until the metal tongue holds still
among its metal teeth and then once more
it winches what won't move to what now will.

Each poem begins where steady turns to whim
when workaday is boring as a fence.
A poem's a maybe mired in now, a song
that plows alone until I come along
to harness up the mental tools I own
and word by word, pull the poem home.

II.

Office Supplies

Covid restrictions may apply

ebook

I stopped touching people last spring.
Then, I still believed there was nothing
much to worry about. *Wash my hands*
while I sing Happy Birthday twice and
don't touch my face. Limit my circle
of contacts to family. My work will
be done from my home, virtually.
I worked, gardened, felt fine until I
ran out of library books too soon.

I own rooms of books, but being doomed
to read old words when I need fresh worlds
made me weary of choices that whirled
from no to no, so I lit a screen
that called itself Book. I said maybe
this will do, and it did, until time
to view page three. I tapped; it flipped. I'm
done. I pulled a book from my bookcase
just to touch the pages, as smooth as
linens at past lunches with friends, our hands
passing food, touching, because we can.

Thumb Drive

It's my cyber suitcase. I keep it stashed
where I could snatch it up, first and fast,
if we evacuate some midnight.
Readiness seems a habit that might
prove more heroic than neurotic.
I could be the savior of: Dog Pics
65-Word Bio   Shopping List
Christmas Card Poem 2006
Postcard Mailing Labels   Phone Contacts
Author Checklist   New Phone Contacts.
"New" because if I delete my friends
who've died, I'll conjure a second end
more final than their first. It's our past
I'm saving to a digital black hole
where all our lives are collapsible
to a tool no larger than my thumb—
which lately has outworked my mind's numb
doom-scrolling through each day's dire warnings
of what more we could lose by morning.

Emoji

Prevent the spread of Covid-19
Wash your hands

Wear a mask
Practice social distancing

We're out of useful emojis here
in the Deep South of my raising where
we hug so natively that when I
was a little girl who didn't like
hostessing my space, Mama used to
tease me the way southern mothers do
to gently make her cast-iron words
stick with me: *You hug like it hurts.*

Never wanting to hurt my mother,
I practiced relaxing to her hugs
until one day mid-hug I got it—
a hug is a gift you get back if
you give it away. These days, we raise
our forgetful arms to touchless space,
the safe air between our flapping hands
a meme for what we want to give but can't.

Text

Like those notes we passed in second grade,
our syntax limited by the space
available on paper folded
four times over so we could hold it
caught by our fingers in the hollows
of small palms as it followed
our whispered directive up the row
to our best friend: *he likes me yes no.*

Now we hold this tablet in both hands
while we type with our thumbs and hit *send,*
our keyboarded directive to slip
our note past those who'd intercept it
if they could. Every text is a prayer
to faceless gods of internet air
for traveling mercies, our reply
an exhalation of anxiety

over things unseen we've gotten adept
at accepting, mostly. Nothing left
to do but hope once it's sent. Isn't that
always the way of things? We set
the course of our days as if intent
were sacrosanct, as if wanting meant
having. Everything's out of our reach
except the perfect *yes* of belief.

Zoom

I am captain of *The Enterprise.*
If my shuttlecraft crew has survived
since yesterday, they'll log in with me
at 0900 hours. Maybe
they've made it past the cosmic dust field
we've been warned about. Maybe we'll just
share updates as if that death cloud
wasn't even now drifting around
heedless of how much I need them alive.

This is how it feels to teach online
during a pandemic. Students zoom
to my screen from their alien homes.
I don't want to see their dogs, their beds.
the close-ups of the tops of their heads
as they adjust their video. We can't
adjust such depthless space. I want to
damn the danger, call them in, sit tight
together through this horizonless night.

Scanner

I sense before I see. Not their color,
but what someone's eyes are searching for,
their light scanning for the right surface
to reflect on. Sometimes it's my face
that catches their question. It's always
a question, isn't it? Their eyes say,
There you are. *Where were you?* It stops me
every time, a fractional hitch we
both expect and don't much think about
except to know when it passes, smoothed out
when I meet their eyes, brown with worry
or the blue of fathomless sorrow.

Photoshop

This is what a pandemic looks like
to students who write their answers when I
ask them what they will most remember:

How we sit with our kids for dinner
every night, all the family.
We never been so close. Sometimes we
hear somebody we know who get sick,
so we just stay home. I ask my kid
if she scared. She say not really, more
just bored/ It like war, you know, Teacher?
A whole lot waiting around. You tell
your kids it's okay, you tell yourself.
You believe it 'cause it too quiet
everywhere. Quiet is good, right?
Then my friend's abuelita dying.
In her house, all the people crying.

I tell them what I'll remember most
is the silence. No cars on our roads.
We could have hop-scotched the center line
like kids, no sounds ahead or behind,
just a warming April sun and our days
as boundless as dreams.

Pandora

All singing is a gift. Silencing
a song stops our breath from travelling
unhindered beyond where hands can touch
or need can claim. Think of how we clutch
the hands of the dying as if we
were holding life itself and could keep
it from leaving by tightening our grip.
Let go. Sing. I have seen my own mother slip
morning by morning past full waking,
shaking her head, no, until, taking
her curled hand in mine to insist her
once more to my bewildering world,
I led her into song. Easing, she heard
her name on every note and answered,
I remember.

Alexa

Faith is the substance of things hoped for, the
evidence of things not seen. Hebrews 11:1

Alexa, do you believe in ghosts?
Do unseen phantoms doom us? No, hush—
I know you can't answer this except
politely, as we've come to expect
of you, our digital concierge,
our Lady of Fulfillment. If there's
an unanswerable flung your way
in jest or desperation, you say
you're sorry but you cannot provide
that information. It's okay. I'd
rather wonder what my chances are
to keep escaping these zombie germs
than be mollified that all of us
will be well, despite the obvious.

Google

Everything I have no need to know
scrolls out like ancient scripture below
my inquiry. I let myself digress
to the almost-useful, to the less-
than-helpful, the beguiling lure
of related quandaries' answers,
but not my own. So much pleasanter
to stroll along these paths to other
resolutions than be stopped by fact
as it relates to me—then have to act.

GPS

God paused society. Said, "Hold still,
you're dirty. Don't you dare move. Let's see
if I can find a way to clean you up.
Be right back." We waited all summer
and into the fall. Hunkering down,
days blew from our hands like seeds. The ground
grew thickety with minutes
we knew no way to spend except in
being there. A novelty of time
kept us amused. None of us had seen
a greening lovelier. But August
wearied us, its heat and sameness just
too much. We grew willing to wander
any path to get to September.

Password

The keys to a digital kingdom
are mine if I find where I hid them.
Some faceless gatekeeper tells me he's
sorry, but my password seems to be
incorrect. Try again. I'm locked out of
my own cyber house, banned, in spite of
obviously owning the fingers
which coded-in yesterday after
three false tries and I'm Not a Robot
validation. Passcodes I forgot
I once knew saunter past, taunting me
with hints each might be the missing key.

I wake each day and the world has changed,
but I haven't. Rising, I manage
my constants: feed the cats, water the fern,
sweep out the house. The ready comfort
of caretaking steadies me. Green tea,
the side porch, a colander of peas
to shell while Ginger and Chloe purr
in Mama's rocker. Naming my world
brings it to me as it was before
someone somewhere last night closed a door
carefully, mostly muffling the click
of their key in a gradual lock.

Dark Web

A moonless night and a forest path
you know better than to follow, yet
a steady creep of hooded others
comes to wander here, and the wonder
of it is that more aren't lured by lust
to plunder, or driven by disgust
to try to confound what can't be killed:
this web that shifts like a virus, still
strong, always plotting a new path.

Malware

Silently it slips inside your world
and subtly alters you. It unfurls
what's permissible, leaves you flapping
in a gasp of disbelief that things
could go so deeply wrong. Scared to touch
where yesterday you laid claim, so much
now out of your hands, nothing to do
but nothing. Meanwhile, a virus you
can't quite believe in is busy raiding
the storage boxes of your past, trading
on your refusal to name what you
can't fight, to confront would make it true.

Delete

Don't you wish you could hit delete
to clear your memory? How neat
and brief that year's cached days would be
minus the virus that suddenly
ransomed everyone you need,
including yourself, but chose to keep
a few, including yourself, or
at least the *you* you were before
it wasn't safe to breathe or touch,
which made you want to hug so much
you'd try to sneak a quick one past
the invisibles. Good luck with that.
Everyone's caught something
that has left a scar. If there's one thing
to be said for fleeing death, it's
that you stockpile some good stories.
Save them. Bring them out when the long
night ends and it's time for a song.

III.

Tools for Mind and Body

Some templates to try

Coping Mechanism

Past midnight. Time to move inside.
She's asleep, doors locked,
the curtains drawn, all the lights
darkened. She's forgotten

she can't lock herself, though.
Just the opposite.
Her eyes close, her breathing slows,
neurons ease and slip

from listening to resting mode.
All defenses down.
Or are they? She begins to moan,
tossing, restless now.

Her dreaming shifts to half-aware,
something isn't right.
She rises, seamless as a prayer,
to listen to the night

and get her bearings. Waiting there,
not to fight,
but to refuse whatever
has arrived.

She's learned not to answer when
destruction knocks.
She's learned to trust her permanence,
even though it's not.

    —Covid-19, virus

Patience

He'd never talked to me before
that day at lunch. He said,
That year I waited by the door.
I'd wake, get out of bed,

get dressed, go out and sit and watch
the people passing by.
I noticed how they moved. I watched
their faces, studied eyes,

their mouths. I taught myself to walk
the way they walked, to raise
my hand hello, to nod and talk
a bit about the day's

worrisome drought or gully washer.
Last light, I'd head inside
to eat, to read. Darkness ushered
in the dreams again, so, first light,

I'd start all over. After a year
or so, I passed right well.
There he stopped, tipped back his chair.
Nothing else to tell.

Long time coming home from war,
I asked? He nodded *yes,*
studied me a moment more,
picked up his plate and left.

—James Still, writer, U.S. Army, WWII

Storytelling

She got my goat. All that crap
about listening for
her muse, about needing to tap
some mystic artistic source

of inspiration. I'm guessing she's
never been truly poor.
I write to feed my family,
I told her. Nothing is more

inspiring than four bellies to fill.
Now, this in no way implies
my books aren't written well. People,
I am eleventh of twelve

reared on a farm in Vanna, Georgia.
You think I didn't learn
early on to do my chores
right and regular

just to keep the farm alive?
I've gotta tell you, though,
sometimes when brother John and I
had weeded the last row,

we'd grin and race each other home,
the sweat work all behind us,
the smells of supper on the stove.
No way in hell you'll find

truer inspiration than work,
hard work. Plant your story
on a page. It's yours,
but not until you earn it.

—*Terry Kay, storyteller, mentor*

Comfort

Hey, buddy, you know what I really like?
Waking up, then going
right back to sleep. It's mighty fine,
waking up and knowing

you don't have to. I've been yanked
from the arms of Morpheus
by cops, by fire, by every angry
woman east of Jesus.

I get up, pull on my pants, and deal.
When trouble finds you at night,
it's always personal. Can't heal
something I didn't do right

if I had no idea I was doing it wrong.
But I never run. The least
I can do is listen. I get along
by getting along. Jeez Louise,

I hate to fight. Except when trouble's
visiting some family
who just need a night's sleep but all hell's
infesting their life and land.

Injustice riles me. I can see it plain
when it happens to somebody else
and, buddy, I start talking then,
for them, not for myself.

Guess I'm best at standing up
for whoever's not me. Or
maybe I just get tired. That's what
beer and sleep are for.

All I ask for myself is a cold,
refreshing beverage
to mellow me. And my pillow,
the sweetest woman I've had.

—*James Watson Webb, activist poet*

Courage

"We'll get to the tequila store,
but first I want to visit
some migrants waiting at the border
for asylum. They have to sit

by the gate until their number's called.
If they leave, they lose
their place in line." Their kids all
swarm around Peg. She lets them choose

a coloring book, chats with them
while their *mamás* keep vigil
with American air less than
two breaths away. "We'll

be back," Peg tells them, "but I hope you won't."
Pancho hails us, "*Hola*,
Peg!" Pancho's one of those
who didn't know he was

illegal until a traffic ticket
sent him to Mexico.
"We got to move two sisters
to the shelter. You know,

they too young to stay alone.
I need you to come." We climb onboard.
"*Tu eres muy brava*," Peg smiles.
"No," They claim their words,
"*Valiente*." As miles

pile up on miles, I start to fret.
"If Pancho died on us,"—
he grins and mimes dramatic death—
"could you get us home?"

"Nope," Peg sounds so blasé
it settles me.
No soy tan valiente
como ellas. When we

arrive at the shelter, two brisk *damas*
herd the girls with care
and fierceness, exactly what
they need. "Now where?"

Peg grins at me, "Tequila, girl!"
Later, at the gate,
I claim the liquor. "It's not worth
the hassle," Peg says. "Some agents hate

me enough to crucify me for legal
tequila." We make
good time going home. "Well,"
Peg opens one, "Here you go. Take

a shot of courage." Our glasses clink.
It burns like rage. *This*
comes a little late for me, I think,
and you never needed it.

—Peg Bowden, *immigration activist*
Pancho Olachea Martin, *humanitarian*
Unnumbered asylum seekers, *human*

Sight

You're fey, of course. Bound to be—
Irish on both sides,
Patten and Tierney, and Daddy could *see*.
It's why he drank. Besides,

as soon as you decided to talk
when you were nearly two,
you said things you really ought not
know at only two.

They told me before I came here,
you'd answer when I asked,
as if I'd know who *They* were.
I watched you after that

because of Daddy, but you were fine
until you weren't. You'd dream
about a friend and call to find—
sure enough—something

was going wrong with her. You thought
her rough spot was yours
since you could see it, but it's not.
Honey, maybe by now you've learned

you just can't carry all the hurt
in the world. Now I don't mean to
pretend it isn't there, but your
job should be to clean

it up and make it usable,
then move on. The trash
that gets dumped along our road? We haul
off what's no good and stash

the treasures—two-by-fours, a sink,
kittens—until we find
a home for them. Sweetheart, I think
every time you write

a poem you're finding a home for grief,
stitching it like squares
for a quilt. Your grandmother couldn't *see,*
but she could quilt, so there's

your inheritance: Your hands
write poems to balance
your mind in a way your granddaddy
couldn't. You're lucky, Hon.

     —Grace Patten Scoates McCurley, life coach

Silence

He isn't silent. He just can't speak.
Easier if he were both
or neither. Easier for me,
I mean. To tell the truth,

his happy-seeming squeals and *ahhs*
make me clench my teeth.
I wince, my gut goes tight, because
what if I, if we,

if even his caregivers hear him wrong?
What if he intends
his grin to be a grimace? How long
might he have tried to send

a message from his lexicon?
Does he have one? Have we
dismissed as gibberish his one
plea? *I'm here. Hear me.*

It's not being sure that waylays me.
I'm a woman of words.
If he had words to say what he
needs, I could answer.

Or if his language were silence, I'd
keep him company
under his vast and soundless sky.
I am a woman at ease

with silence that rests beneath words.
He has neither and both.
His birth-bound tongue smothers
possible language, but ghostly

exhales of silence whistle free.
He isn't free. Nor I.
I'm useless from pain I can't relieve.
Not his. Mine.

—*Punkin, unknown after twenty years of knowing*

Prayer

And if I am a Christian, I am
the least of all. Well, that's
for sure. I love these words in Romans:
neither death nor life,

nor angels nor demons not as a verse
affirming my faith, but I love
them for sounding like Poe: *Neither*
angels in heaven above,

nor demons down under the sea.
Also, I am convinced
that hell's not a place, but a journey,
heaven's not earned, but spent,

and prayer's another name for song.
Demons dither when
I pray unceasingly through song.
I am persuaded that when

I die, the best of me will drone
eternally in tune
with gratitude for every song
I've ever sung.

—Dana Wildsmith, alto

Acknowledgments

Grateful thanks to the editors of the following publications, where some of these poems first appeared:

Appalachian Journal: "How to Sing," "Sling Blade"
Appalachian Review: "Garden Hoe"
Black Moon Magazine: "Malware," "Password"
Cutleaf Journal: "Door," "Prayer"
Grand Little Things: "History"
Oconee Cultural Arts Foundation's Small Works exhibit: "Password"
Pine Mountain Sand & Gravel: "Seam Ripper"
Songs of Eretz Poetry Review: "Comealong"
The Women of Appalachia Project's anthology *Women Speak*, Volume 7 (Sheila-Na-Gig Editions, 2021): "Patience"

And with deep gratitude to Matthew Teutsch and The Lillian E. Smith Center for residencies during the writing of these poems.

About the Author

Dana Wildsmith is the author of six collections of poetry, a novel, *Jumping*, and an environmental memoir, *Back to Abnormal: Surviving with an Old Farm in the New South*, which was the finalist for Georgia Author of the Year. Wildsmith has served as Artist-in-Residence for Devils Tower National Park, Grand Canyon National Park, and Everglades National Park. She is a Fellow of the Hambidge Center for Science and Creative Arts. Wildsmith works as an English literacy instructor for Lanier Technical College. She lives with her husband on an old farm in the toe of the Appalachians.

CPSIA information can be obtained
at www.ICGtesting.com
Printed in the USA
JSHW022019250523
42280JS00003B/228